MW01504104

Original title:
Shared Radiance

Author: Kene Elistrand
ISBN HARDBACK: 978-1-80560-106-7
ISBN PAPERBACK: 978-1-80560-571-3

The Brilliance of Us

In the day where shadows play,
We find our light, our own ballet.
With every laugh, with every glance,
Together we weave a vibrant dance.

Through whispers soft and dreams aligned,
In the heartbeat of love, we're intertwined.
With every step, with every trust,
We paint the world, it's truly just.

In the chaos, we stand tall,
A united front, we'll never fall.
Through storms we weather, hand in hand,
Our brilliance shines, forever grand.

When darkness threatens to take flight,
Our spark ignites, igniting night.
In silence shared, our souls ignite,
Together we glow, a guiding light.

So let us roam where wonders bloom,
For in your eyes, I see the room.
A place of joy, of dreams to trust,
Forever bound, it's the brilliance of us.

Illuminated by Connection

In twilight's hue, our spirits rise,
A bond unbroken, no disguise.
With every heartbeat, we will find,
The heartfelt ties that bind our minds.

Through laughter shared, our hearts expand,
In gentle moments, we take a stand.
With words unspoken, we understand,
Illuminated, hand in hand.

In shared adventures, side by side,
Through bustling streets, our hearts abide.
The world fades out; it's you and me,
A radiant glow, wild and free.

In every glance, there's truth we see,
Connection strong, like roots of a tree.
Through life's challenges, we will soar,
Together forever, we'll explore.

So here we are, with spirits bright,
In every shadow, we find the light.
Illuminated by love's affection,
Our journey shines, a bold connection.

A Dance of Light

In twilight's glow, we twirl around,
Soft whispers of dusk, sweetly profound.
Stars begin to peek, one by one,
A gentle embrace, two souls as one.

With rays of gold, the horizon kissed,
Each flicker of flame, a moment missed.
In the night's cradle, shadows will play,
Guiding our steps in a luminous ballet.

Celestial Bonds

Under the vastness, we drift and sway,
Galaxies twist in a cosmic ballet.
Linked by stardust, a thread so fine,
Eternal connections, your heart in mine.

Time bends around us, a spiral of light,
Whirling through dreams in the velvet night.
Each pulse of the universe, a silent cue,
Echoes of love in the skies so blue.

The Warmth We Share

Amidst the chill, your smile ignites,
A beacon of warmth on cold, dark nights.
Hands intertwined, the world fades away,
In your embrace, forever I'll stay.

Laughter like sunlight, brightens the day,
Through trials we wander, come what may.
With whispered secrets, our hearts will bloom,
A garden of memories, forever in tune.

Bathed in Light

Morning breaks gently, a canvas anew,
Painting the skies in radiant hue.
Beams of the sun dance on the leaves,
Nature awakens, and my spirit believes.

Wrapped in this glow, sorrows take flight,
Each ray a promise, a gift of delight.
Together we bask, in warmth we reside,
The world in our hearts, forever our guide.

Celestial Celebrations

Stars align in the night,
Dancing with pure delight.
Moonlight casts its soft glow,
Whispers of dreams that flow.

Joyful hearts lift and sing,
In the warmth of spring.
Wishes on stars take flight,
Embracing the starlit night.

Galaxies twirl in grace,
Each a bright, shining face.
Celestial bodies sway,
Marking the night as play.

With laughter and delight,
We share the cosmic light.
Boundless wonders unfold,
In stories yet untold.

Under the night's embrace,
Time finds its sacred place.
In this vast, endless sea,
We find our unity.

Radiating Affection

Sunrise paints the sky red,
Soft whispers gently spread.
Warmth of love fills the air,
Embraces beyond compare.

Hearts beat in sweet refrain,
Dancing through joy and pain.
In each glance, sparks ignite,
Binding souls in pure light.

Hands held in silent peace,
Every worry finds release.
Gentle words like a song,
In their rhythm, we belong.

With every laugh, we grow,
In the warmth of love's glow.
Moments like stars align,
Radiate, pure and divine.

Eternal love, our guide,
With you always by my side.
Through seasons, we will shine,
Forever, your heart is mine.

A Coalition of Rays

Sunbeams pierce through the trees,
Kissing the earth with ease.
Shadows dance in the light,
Creating beauty from sight.

With colors bright and bold,
Nature's canvas unfolds.
Every leaf soft and bright,
Sharing joy, pure delight.

Gathered rays come alive,
In symphonies they thrive.
Together, bright and strong,
Turning sorrow to song.

Each spark a guiding star,
Near or ever so far.
Together, hand in hand,
We create our own land.

In this coalition blessed,
Love shines forth, never stressed.
Unity, our strong base,
Illuminates every place.

Light Weaving Dreams

Threads of gold in the sky,
Stitching hopes that soar high.
Each dream a radiant beam,
Crafting life's gentle scheme.

Weaving visions of splendor,
In hearts' chambers, we render.
With each whisper and sigh,
Our aspirations can fly.

Particles swirl and twirl,
In the dance, dreams unfurl.
Underneath the starlit seam,
We navigate each sweet dream.

In the dawn, colors blend,
Promises we'll always send.
Together, let us gleam,
In the fabric of a dream.

With each spark, we ignite,
Guiding through darkest night.
In this tapestry, we share,
A lifetime of love and care.

Illuminated Journeys

Through the shadows we will stride,
With our dreams as our guide.
Every step a story holds,
In the light, our hearts unfold.

Paths unwinding in the night,
Chasing stars, embracing light.
In pursuit of what's unknown,
Together, we have always grown.

Mountains high and valleys wide,
With courage as our pride.
Every mile a memory made,
In the light, our fears will fade.

Winding roads beneath the moon,
In harmony, we find the tune.
Each adventure, a chance to learn,
With every twist, the fire will burn.

Brighter tomorrows lie ahead,
In the light, no tears unshed.
Hand in hand, we'll face the dawn,
On this journey, we've moved on.

The Warmth of Togetherness

Gather close, let spirits blend,
In this moment, hearts transcend.
Fires crackle, laughter spreads,
With each word, a love that spreads.

In the cozy evening glow,
Time slows down, emotions flow.
Wrapped in warmth, a shared embrace,
Together, we have found our place.

In quiet talks and playful games,
We weave stories, share our names.
Finding joy in simple things,
In this bond, our spirit sings.

As seasons change and days drift by,
With every moment, we learn to fly.
Hand in hand through thick and thin,
In togetherness, we always win.

So here's to love and trust, our creed,
In our hearts, we plant the seed.
Together, we will always stand,
In the warmth of this wonderland.

Consortium of Light

In the gathering of bright souls,
We ignite the fire that rolls.
With each spark, we find our place,
In unity, we share our grace.

Dancing beams of hope and cheer,
In this chorus, we have no fear.
Light connects us, near and far,
In this grand celestial spar.

Voices blend in harmony,
A radiant, strong symphony.
Together, we will shine so bright,
In our hearts, a flame of light.

Through the storms and endless night,
We will stand with all our might.
Hand in hand, we will unite,
Creating our consortium of light.

With every dream that we ignite,
In this journey, we share our sight.
Together, we embrace the glow,
In our hearts, the love will grow.

Sparked by Unity

From separate paths, we did emerge,
In harmony, we find the surge.
With every laugh, and every tear,
We rise together, far and near.

In times of struggle, hearts align,
With every challenge, we boldly shine.
Each moment shared, a chance to grow,
In this bond, our spirits flow.

As we weave through life's great dance,
We find power in every chance.
With hands united, dreams take flight,
In the unity, we find our light.

From shared whispers to roaring cheers,
We stand strong against all fears.
In each story, our truth is spun,
Together, we'll always be one.

So here's to the fire in our hearts,
With love's power, we'll never part.
In every moment, let us see,
How beautiful life can truly be.

Embracing Luminescence

In the quiet of night, stars begin to gleam,
Whispers of dreams dance in silver beams.
We journey through shadows, hand in hand,
Embracing the light, a radiant band.

Hope flickers softly, igniting our path,
Guiding us gently, diminishing wrath.
With hearts wide open, we gather the glow,
Embracing the luminescence we sow.

Each moment, a spark, a chance to ignite,
Together we rise, painting the night.
Through darkened valleys, our spirits will climb,
In the glow of our courage, we'll shine every time.

The warmth of connection, pure and sincere,
Banishing doubts, casting away fear.
In the embrace of our love, we'll find
Luminescence eternal, beautifully blind.

The Spark We Create

From ashes of silence, a whisper is born,
A spark in the darkness, a new day's dawn.
Together we forge, with passion and might,
The flame of our fervor, igniting the night.

With every heartbeat, our rhythms align,
Crafting the melody, a journey divine.
United in purpose, our spirits afire,
The spark that we create, lifts us higher.

Like fireworks blooming, we burst into flight,
Chasing our dreams, like stars in the night.
Hand in hand, we traverse the unknown,
In the warmth of our bond, we are never alone.

Together we shine, against trials we fight,
With laughter and love, we joyously light.
Each moment a gift, shared with delight,
The spark we create, our everlasting light.

Illuminated Threads

In the fabric of life, woven so tight,
Are threads of connection, shimmering bright.
Each story a strand, unique yet combined,
Illuminated threads, beautifully entwined.

With each gentle tug, the tapestry grows,
Rich with emotion, the love that it shows.
Through laughter and tears, we stitch and we sew,
Creating a masterpiece, together we glow.

In colors of kindness, compassion and grace,
We brighten the world, a warm, tender place.
As stars in the sky, our spirits ascend,
Illuminated threads, a bond without end.

Celebrating moments, both big and small,
Together we rise, we will never fall.
With hearts intertwined, in harmony led,
The beauty of life, through these threads is spread.

United in Brilliance

In the heart of the storm, we find our way,
United in brilliance, come what may.
With courage as armor, and love as our guide,
Together we flourish, side by side.

Through valleys of shadows, we conquer the night,
Shining like stars, illuminating the fight.
With every heartbeat, with every embrace,
United in brilliance, we carve our own space.

Our laughter's a beacon, our dreams intertwine,
Beneath the same sky, our spirits align.
In moments of doubt, we stand strong and tall,
United in brilliance, we conquer it all.

With love as our compass, we navigate seas,
Finding strength in our bond, a gentle breeze.
Toward horizons unknown, we gracefully sail,
United in brilliance, we will never fail.

A Symphony of Dazzle

In the night sky, stars unfold,
Whispers of dreams, tales of old.
Notes of silence, soft and clear,
In the darkness, beauty near.

Moments twinkle, hearts align,
Dancing shadows, hands entwine.
Harmony in every glance,
Life's enchanting, fleeting dance.

Colors merge in vibrant streams,
Life's a canvas, brushed with dreams.
Echoes linger, fading light,
Chasing shadows, holding tight.

In the stillness, joy takes flight,
Melodies weave through the night.
Symphonies of life embrace,
Leaving memories, warm and grace.

Glows of Companionship

Together we laugh, side by side,
In every moment, joy can't hide.
Through stormy nights and sunny days,
Friendship shines in countless ways.

Shared secrets whispered in the dark,
In your presence, ignites a spark.
Hand in hand, we roam the path,
In your smile, I find my laugh.

Old stories told, like gold they gleam,
Woven memories, a sacred dream.
When shadows loom, we chase the fear,
In unity's glow, all becomes clear.

Through trials faced, we stand our ground,
With every heartbeat, love is found.
A bond like ours, forever stays,
Guided by love through all our days.

Sparks of Connection

In a crowded room, eyes collide,
Silent sparks where hearts confide.
A fleeting glance, a knowing smile,
In that moment, time feels worthwhile.

Bridges built with words unsaid,
Across the gaps, our spirits tread.
Each heartbeat echoes, a soft refrain,
In the web of life, we weave the same.

A touch of hands, a laugh exchanged,
In simple moments, bonds arranged.
Through laughter and tears, we grow,
In every heartbeat, love will flow.

Each connection, a thread so fine,
In life's tapestry, brightly shine.
Every story, woven tight,
In the tapestry, dreams take flight.

In the Light of Kindness

Small gestures bloom, like flowers bright,
In the shadows, a guiding light.
A smile shared, a hand outstretched,
In kindness' glow, hearts are fetched.

Gentle words like whispers soft,
Lift spirits high, where they once loft.
Through tender acts, we break the ice,
In love's embrace, we find our price.

Each moment cherished, love's sweet call,
Together we rise, together we fall.
With open hearts, we pave the way,
In kindness' light, we choose to stay.

Fragments of hope, we weave with care,
In life's embrace, we learn to share.
A simple touch, a heartfelt sign,
In the light of kindness, we all shine.

Reflections in Togetherness

In the mirror of shared smiles,
We find our stories woven tight,
Each laughter echoing for miles,
A tapestry of soft light.

Hands that reach across the years,
Binding hearts in gentle grace,
Through joy, through sorrow, through tears,
Together we find our place.

Footsteps echo on the path,
Every moment, every glance,
Strength in love ignites the math,
Together we dare to dance.

In quiet nights, we share our dreams,
The stars above, our guiding friends,
Reflecting warmth in moonlit beams,
Together, the journey never ends.

Embracing the Dawn

As sun breaks through the silent night,
Soft colors paint the waking sky,
In this moment, hearts take flight,
Embracing all that we can try.

With open arms, we greet the day,
Awakening to hopes anew,
Chasing shadows far away,
Together facing life's debut.

The whispers of the morning breeze,
Carry promise, fresh and bright,
In this harmony, we find ease,
A symphony of pure delight.

Each dawn a canvas for our dreams,
United in the light we share,
Together, stitched through all extremes,
In every sunrise, love laid bare.

Bright Threads of Kinship

Threads of laughter run so deep,
Woven through our tangled tales,
In each bond, a promise keep,
Through the storms, through gentle gales.

Moments shared like rays of light,
Illuminate our winding way,
In this fabric, strong and bright,
Kinship blooms in each array.

With every stitch, a story sewn,
Every heartbeat, every cheer,
In this craft, we are not alone,
Together, we conquer our fear.

Patterns shifting, never lost,
Colors blending, rich and bold,
In the warmth, we bear the cost,
Bright threads of kinship, heart and soul.

Alight with Togetherness

In the glow of fading light,
Together we find our way,
Each moment holds a spark so bright,
Alight with love in the fray.

Around the fire, stories weave,
The flames dance in our delight,
In the warmth, we all believe,
Together, we reach new heights.

The night unfolds with whispered dreams,
Connected by the stars above,
In unity, our spirit gleams,
Together, we share this love.

With every heartbeat, we ignite,
A symphony of shared embrace,
In the shadows, we are the light,
Together, we find our grace.

In the Company of Light

In the dawn's gentle glow,
Shadows softly fade away.
We wander through the day,
Bright whispers lead our way.

Every twinkle tells a tale,
In the air, warmth unfolds.
Hope dances on the breeze,
As new dreams take their hold.

Stars ignite in velvet skies,
Their shine, a fleeting kiss.
In this realm of magic,
We discover simple bliss.

Together, hearts align,
With laughter interlaced.
Let's bask in endless light,
Our spirits interphased.

In the stillness of the night,
With wonders all around,
We find our strength within,
In this love, we are found.

The Spark That Unites

In the quiet of the heart,
A flicker starts to blaze.
Two souls in harmony,
Lost in a joyous daze.

Through adversity, we shine,
With courage as our guide.
The spark ignites the passion,
Together, side by side.

From embers to a flame,
Our spirits intertwine.
Illuminated journey,
In love's sweet, sacred shrine.

With every challenge faced,
Our bond grows ever strong.
In unity, we flourish,
Together we belong.

In moments shared in light,
We spark the world's delight.
A beacon shining bright,
Love's warmth will be our sight.

Chasing Brilliance

Upon the horizon's edge,
Dreams take flight like birds.
In the canvas of the sky,
We paint with vibrant words.

With each step forward, rise,
To catch the fleeting gleam.
Pursuing golden moments,
In the realm of our dream.

Across the mountains high,
In valleys deep and wide,
We chase the light of hope,
With passion as our guide.

Through forests thick and lush,
Under the moon's soft gaze,
We run towards the brilliance,
In life's enchanting maze.

In the glow of twilight,
With stars that start to glow,
We gather all the wonders,
To share and let them flow.

Echoes of Illumination

In the quiet of the night,
Echoes whisper soft and low.
Memories illuminated,
In the heart, they gently flow.

Flickers of the past arise,
Like shadows dancing free.
In the stillness, we can hear,
What the light reveals to me.

Through the corridors of time,
Visions shimmer, pure and grand.
In each echo, we find hope,
A future close at hand.

With the dawn, the echoes fade,
But their warmth will still remain.
In the light of each new day,
We embrace joy, not the pain.

So let us hold these echoes tight,
For they guide us toward the right.
In the dance of light and shade,
We find our truths displayed.

Tapestry of Glow

Threads of gold in the twilight,
Weaving dreams, soft and bright.
Whispers echo in the night,
As stars emerge, a wondrous sight.

Colors blend under the moon,
Creating a peaceful tune.
Nature sings a gentle boon,
In this enchanted afternoon.

Every glow tells a tale,
Of hearts brave, not frail.
Each shimmer like a sail,
Guiding us along the trail.

Woven moments, bonds so tight,
Carried forth with pure delight.
A tapestry that feels just right,
In harmony, we take flight.

With every thread, new stories flow,
In the fabric, love does grow.
A tapestry of warmth and glow,
Shining bright, forever show.

Bonds in the Morning Mist

In the dawn, the mist does rise,
Veiling secrets, painted skies.
Whispers linger, soft surprise,
Where friendship blooms and never dies.

Gentle touches, hearts entwined,
In soft beauty, joy we find.
Through the fog, our paths aligned,
A bond ethereal, truly kind.

Every breath a sacred trust,
In quiet moments, we adjust.
When shadows fall, we know we must,
Stand together, fight, and thrust.

Morning light breaks through the gray,
Guiding friendships on their way.
In the mist, we laugh and play,
Creating memories that will stay.

With each dawn, we rise anew,
In the mist, our dreams pursue.
Bonds unbroken, tried and true,
Forever cherished, me and you.

Dance of the Luminaries

Underneath the starry gleam,
All the luminaries beam.
In the night, they swirl and dream,
Dancing lightly, like a stream.

Flickers of light, hearts combined,
In this waltz, we are aligned.
Guided by the cosmos, blind,
Together, paths we shall find.

Every twinkle a soft sigh,
Whispers echo through the sky.
As the shadows flutter by,
In this dance, we learn to fly.

Galaxies spin and twirl around,
In the silence, love is found.
In this rhythm, we're unbound,
In the night, our souls resound.

Let us dance until the dawn,
In the light, our worries gone.
As the morning breaks upon,
We weave dreams to carry on.

Luminaries Intertwined

In the cosmos, we unite,
With our dreams, we take flight.
Luminaries shining bright,
Illuminating the dark night.

Threads of silver in the air,
Each connection, a silent prayer.
In the beauty, we lay bare,
Hearts entwined without a care.

Cradled by the moon's embrace,
Finding solace in this space.
In the starlight, we find grace,
Together, time we shall trace.

Veils of wonder gently fold,
Stories waiting to be told.
Through the ages, strong and bold,
Our luminaries, never sold.

As the dawn begins to break,
With each moment, memories make.
In this dance, our hearts awake,
Together, our bond we stake.

A Symphony of Brightness

In the morning's gentle glow,
Colors dance, the world in tow.
Birds prepare their sweet delight,
Melodies weave through the light.

Every hue, a note's embrace,
Nature sings with endless grace.
Life unfolds in vibrant rays,
Painting joy in myriad ways.

Laughter fills the crisp, fresh air,
Sunshine glistens on each hair.
Hope awakens with the dawn,
Radiance where the dark has shawn.

The canvas brightens, hearts ignite,
Each soul finds its spark tonight.
Together we ignite the fire,
A symphony that won't expire.

With each moment, colors blend,
In this life, our hearts transcend.
A union forged in bright arrays,
A symphony for all our days.

When Shadows Converge

Beneath the veil of twilight's chord,
Whispers weave where shadows hoard.
Flickers hint of light nearby,
In the dark, our dreams will fly.

Silent secrets start to form,
In the stillness, fears grow warm.
Yet in gloom, we clasp our hands,
Creating worlds, where hope expands.

Stars begin their slow ascent,
In our chest, a fierce lament.
But together, we carve our space,
Finding strength in each embrace.

Time may bend, and darkness fall,
Yet in shadows, we hear the call.
What seems lost may guide the way,
Illuminate the dawn's first gray.

When the night evokes our fears,
And the heart, it pales in tears,
Remember, shadows cannot bind,
But rather bring us to the light.

The Light We Create

With every smile that we share,
We spark a flame, an answered prayer.
In our laughter, shadows break,
A tapestry that we awake.

Hands united, hearts aligned,
Together, magic we will find.
Each moment, like a candle's glow,
Illuminates the path we go.

In quiet rooms where dreams unfold,
Stories linger, love retold.
In every hug, a warmth we share,
Guiding souls with tender care.

We are the architects of light,
Building bridges, taking flight.
In each encounter, we embrace,
The beauty of this sacred space.

Through storm and strife, we will thrive,
In the kindness, we come alive.
Creating worlds where hope takes shape,
For in our hands, the light we make.

Radiant Conversations

Words like petals softly fall,
Caressing hearts, we heed the call.
In every exchange, a story shared,
Connection grows, we are prepared.

As voices blend in softest tones,
The warmth of trust, it brightly shone.
Gentle laughter, moments bright,
Illuminate the long, dark night.

Each dialogue, a dance divine,
We trace our paths where souls entwine.
Listening deep, we grow and learn,
Through words, a sacred fire will burn.

In silence too, we find our grace,
In every pause, a sacred space.
What is spoken, yet unexpressed,
Unfolds a truth, deeply blessed.

Radiant hearts in endless talk,
Building bridges as we walk.
In every conversation's spark,
We find the light within the dark.

The Flicker of Together

In the twilight's soft embrace,
We share a fleeting glance.
Hearts beating in gentle rhythm,
A dance of silent chance.

Underneath the starry glow,
Whispers float on the night air.
Unified by secrets kept,
In moments we both share.

Every flicker, every spark,
A testament of our bond.
Through shadows, through the light,
In each twilight, we respond.

Holding hands through shifting tides,
Guided by the moon's embrace.
Together we navigate,
This vast, enchanted space.

In the quiet, in the noise,
We find our own sweet song.
The flicker of togetherness,
A place where we belong.

Celestial Harmony

Beneath the vast and stellar skies,
We dance with dreams unbound.
A symphony of quiet stars,
Celestial truths profound.

Each note in perfect unity,
As planets spin and glide.
The cosmos hums a melody,
In which our hopes reside.

Galaxies collide in grace,
Creating vibrant hues.
The harmony of the heavens,
A canvas we can choose.

Through orbits of our passion,
We travel side by side.
In this celestial embrace,
Our spirits soar and glide.

With every beat, a promise,
To cherish what we find.
In the symphony of stardust,
Our hearts forever bind.

Bridging Brilliance

Across the chasm, light descends,
Creating paths anew.
We build with threads of yesterday,
Unraveling the blue.

Each spark a bridge between us,
Connecting hearts and minds.
In the glow of shared endeavors,
A brilliance that unwinds.

We traverse through the silence,
With courage as our guide.
Bridging gaps of understanding,
With truth we cannot hide.

With every step, we rise above,
Illuminating the way.
In harmony, we're stronger,
Together here we'll stay.

As dawn ignites the horizon,
We carve our dreams in light.
Bridging brilliance in the heart,
Our future shining bright.

The Pulse of Illumination

In shadows cast by fading night,
We find the pulse of light.
With every heartbeat we embrace,
A glow that feels so right.

Through journeys both near and far,
Illumination guides our path.
The rhythm of our shared existence,
In every laugh and wrath.

Each ember flickers with intent,
A spark of hope we cherish.
In the dance of day and night,
Our dreams will never perish.

The pulse of warmth within our souls,
A beacon in the dark.
Together we'll embrace the dawn,
With love, we leave our mark.

With every moment intertwined,
Our spirits intertwined.
In the pulse of illumination,
Endless wonders, we shall find.

The Warmth We Carry

In the quiet of the night,
Whispers of love ignite,
Hearts entwined, so bright,
We hold each other tight.

Memories of laughter play,
Soft echoes in the day,
Through shadows, we will sway,
Chasing fears away.

A fire within us glows,
Wherever the journey goes,
Comfort in what we chose,
Through changes, love grows.

With every step we take,
In moments that we make,
A bond that will not break,
For warmth is ours to stake.

Together, we will stand,
With dreams all well-planned,
Through storms, we command,
A future so grand.

Synchronicity of Stars

Beneath the vast, dark sky,
Stars twinkle, dreams fly high,
Each point a silent sigh,
In cosmic lullabies.

Guided by their bright light,
We wander through the night,
In awe of such pure sight,
Together, futures bright.

Moments weave like a thread,
In paths where dreams are led,
In silence, words unsaid,
By starlight, we are fed.

Connections intertwined,
In constellations aligned,
With fate, our hearts designed,
In time, forever bind.

The universe, vast and wide,
In stellar arms, we glide,
Through the cosmos, we bide,
With love as our guide.

Flickers of Understanding

In the stillness, we find,
Flickers of shared mind,
With hearts so intertwined,
In silence, kind.

A glance, a knowing smile,
Communication, so worthwhile,
Bridges built through every mile,
Together, we compile.

In moments soft and rare,
We uncover truths laid bare,
Depth of feeling, mutual care,
Connection beyond compare.

Tides of thought ebb and flow,
In light, we let our feelings show,
With every spark that we sow,
Understanding starts to grow.

Through the chaos, we see,
The beauty of you and me,
In unity, we break free,
Crafting our own decree.

Luminescent Souls

In the dark, a glow ignites,
Souls leap into the nights,
With every breath, we write,
A dance of pure delights.

Radiance in each embrace,
Shining with endless grace,
Together, we mark our space,
In love's warm, bright chase.

Each heartbeat is a song,
In harmony, we belong,
Through trials, we grow strong,
In light, we carry on.

Luminescent paths we tread,
With every word unsaid,
In dreams where we are led,
In hopes, we're gently fed.

Through the veil, we can see,
A world of possibility,
With hearts in unity,
Our future's tapestry.

Radiant Echoes

In the heart of the night, it shines,
A whisper of hope, soft designs.
Echoes of laughter, joy untold,
Memories cherished, hearts unfold.

Glimmers of dreams dance through the air,
Bringing warmth to souls laid bare.
Together we rise, hand in hand,
In unison, we take our stand.

Through shadows that linger, we will glide,
With radiant echoes, side by side.
Each beat a promise, a sweet refrain,
In harmony, we break the chains.

Stars above witness our flight,
Illuminated paths, pure delight.
Together we weave, a tapestry bright,
Filling the world with shimmering light.

In every heart, a flame we keep,
In silent vows, our spirits leap.
Radiant echoes forever ring,
In the dance of life, we sing.

The Glow of Togetherness

In every smile, a spark ignites,
Illuminating the darkest nights.
Shared laughter lingers in the air,
A bond of love, beyond compare.

Holding hands through trials we face,
Finding strength in this sacred space.
Together we shelter from the storm,
Embracing the beauty of being warm.

In quiet moments, our hearts converse,
A glow of togetherness, our universe.
Through every challenge, we will prevail,
With love as our compass, we shall sail.

Each sunset we watch, painted in gold,
Stories of us whispered and told.
Together we rise, like the morning sun,
Forever bound, our hearts as one.

In the glow of twilight, hand in hand,
We walk this journey, forever we'll stand.
A radiant promise, steadfast and true,
In every moment, I cherish you.

Light as One

When footsteps align, and hearts collide,
We shine like stars, a cosmic guide.
United in purpose, strong and free,
In the dance of life, just you and me.

With every heartbeat, our essence blends,
Creating a light that never ends.
In laughter and tears, we find our way,
Illuminating paths, come what may.

Through the fog of doubt, we choose to rise,
A beacon of hope in the boundless skies.
With unity as our treasured role,
Together we light up every soul.

In moments of silence, we can hear,
The whispers of love drawing us near.
Hand in hand, we traverse the night,
Woven together, our spirits ignite.

Light as one, we bridge the divide,
With hearts entwined, we won't hide.
In the tapestry of life, brightly spun,
Our love is the thread that connects as one.

Constellations of Kindred Spirits

In the night sky, we find our place,
Constellations born from love and grace.
Guiding each other through lost and found,
Bonds unbroken, forever unbound.

With every heartbeat, a star is born,
Shedding light on the path we've worn.
In laughter and whispers, our souls entwined,
A universe built in hearts and minds.

Through tides of time, our spirits soar,
A celestial embrace that we adore.
Together we chart the vast unknown,
In the glow of friendship, we have grown.

Every moment shared, a shimmering thread,
In the fabric of life, where love is spread.
Kindred spirits, in harmony sing,
A melody sweet, through everything.

As constellations light up the night,
We shine ever brighter, a beautiful sight.
In the vast cosmos, we find our way,
Together forever, come what may.

Celebrating Luminosity

In the night, stars gleam bright,
Each spark a story, shining light.
Colors dance in skies so wide,
In this moment, hearts collide.

Voices rise in joyful song,
Together, we all belong.
Echoes of laughter fill the air,
In unity, we truly care.

Waves of warmth, a gentle breeze,
Nature whispers through the trees.
Together, our spirits soar,
In this glow, we seek for more.

Time stands still, a captured bliss,
In every smile, a fleeting kiss.
Glimmers of hope, a guiding flame,
In this circle, we are the same.

As the dawn begins to break,
We celebrate the paths we make.
Hand in hand, we face the day,
In our hearts, we'll find our way.

The Glow of Connection

Fingers traced on weary skin,
A spark ignites, a light within.
In quiet moments, bonds are formed,
In shared silence, we are warmed.

Eyes that meet, a spark so rare,
In the stillness, we find care.
A simple touch, a glance exchanged,
In this dance, we are unchanged.

Every heartbeat, a soft refrain,
Each memory holds joy and pain.
Laughter echoes through the night,
In connections, we find our light.

Time may fade, but we remain,
In this glow, there is no pain.
Through challenges, we find our way,
Creating bonds that never sway.

With open hearts, we journey on,
In every dusk, there lies a dawn.
Together we rise, stronger still,
In this glow, we find our will.

Radiant Togetherness

Hand in hand, we light the way,
With laughter's echo, come what may.
In the warmth of friends so dear,
Together, all our paths are clear.

A tapestry of dreams we weave,
In shared hopes, we truly believe.
Colors blend, a vivid scene,
In this bond, we create the serene.

As shadows fade and daylight breaks,
In unity, the world awakes.
Every smile, a spark ignites,
In togetherness, we find our rights.

Through the storms, we bravely stand,
In this haven, we're hand in hand.
Every trial, a story affirms,
In the light, our spirit warms.

Together, we chase the sun,
In our laughter, many become one.
A radiant heart forever glows,
In this togetherness, love grows.

Flickers of Mutual Light

In the quiet, a flicker shines,
Two souls meet in gentle lines.
Through the haze, a path we find,
In every heartbeat, hearts aligned.

Starlit skies weave stories bright,
With every glance, we share the night.
Echoes linger, soft and sweet,
In this moment, love's heartbeat.

Warmth surrounds like a soft glow,
In every whisper, we come to know.
Through the shadows, laughter gleams,
Building up our cherished dreams.

Flickers dance in the twilight air,
With open hearts, we boldly share.
Every smile, a light in dark,
In this embrace, we leave our mark.

Trust in the fire that burns so bright,
In this connection, we ignite.
With every breath, we rise anew,
In mutual light, we live true.

Surrounding Gleam

In twilight's embrace, soft light breaks,
Whispers of the night, gentle aches.
Stars peek through the velvet haze,
Illuminating our secret ways.

The moonlight dances on the trees,
Carrying a song upon the breeze.
Shadows blend, entwined with grace,
Holding warmth in this sacred space.

Through pathways lined with silver threads,
A tapestry, where magic spreads.
Hearts entwined, in silent dreams,
We gather solace in the gleams.

Moments linger, softly spun,
Like threads of gold beneath the sun.
In every glance, a spark ignites,
Reflecting love in endless nights.

Together, we chase the twilight glow,
Painting memories in colors flow.
The surrounding gleam, a cherished sight,
Guides us through the fabric of night.

The Glow We Nurture

In the heart of night, a fire glows,
Embers whisper tales the darkness knows.
Together we stand, hand in hand,
A warmth that flows, a sacred strand.

With every laugh, the light expands,
Casting shadows, where joy withstands.
Through trials faced, our strength reborn,
In the glow, our spirits adorn.

Moments woven, a delicate lace,
In each heartbeat, a sacred place.
The glow we nurture, fierce and bright,
Guides our souls in the endless night.

Beneath the sky, a tapestry spun,
Together we shine, two hearts as one.
With every tear, a lesson learned,
In the glow of love, forever turned.

As dawn approaches, the stars will fade,
But in our hearts, the glow won't trade.
In every sunrise, a promise made,
The warmth of our bond will never jade.

Illuminative Confluence

In shadows deep, our circles meet,
A crossroads bright with hearts entreat.
The flow of dreams, a tangible stream,
In the illuminative confluence, we teem.

Voices merge like rivers collide,
Creating a harmony, side by side.
With eyes alight, the world expands,
Crafting moments that time demands.

Each story shared, a candle's spark,
Guides us through this endless dark.
In vibrant colors, we paint our fate,
A tapestry woven, love radiates.

Hand in hand, we rise and fall,
Through every echo, we hear the call.
In the dance of life, we intertwine,
A luminous pact that's truly divine.

In unity, we find our strength,
In every heartbeat, a tale at length.
The world transforms, a canvas bright,
In the illuminative confluence of light.

The Essence of Togetherness

In quiet moments, we find our song,
The essence of togetherness, where we belong.
Soft whispers shared beneath the stars,
In each other's presence, we heal our scars.

Through laughter, tears, the seasons roll,
In shared glances, we see the whole.
With every heartbeat, a pulse of trust,
In the essence of love, we find what's just.

Paths may diverge, but hearts remain,
In the bond we forge, through joy and pain.
With open arms, we dare to dream,
Together we rise, a united theme.

In the tapestry of memories spun,
Woven with threads of two becoming one.
Through thick and thin, we hold the flame,
The essence of togetherness, our claim.

As the dawn breaks, our spirits soar,
In each other's hearts, we find the core.
A journey shared, our souls align,
In the essence of love, forever shine.

Unity in Light

In shadows deep, we find our way,
Through trials faced, we learn to stay.
Hand in hand, we rise above,
Bound by strength, united by love.

With every step, we share the glow,
Lighting paths that we both know.
Together we are brave and bold,
Our spirits warm, our hearts of gold.

When storms may come and fears arise,
We stand as one, look to the skies.
With hope as our guiding star,
Together we'll journey, no matter how far.

In laughter shared, in silence too,
In every moment, I see you.
A bond unbreakable, shining bright,
In the tapestry of unity, we find our light.

So let us cherish this sacred thread,
Let love and kindness be widely spread.
For when we stand, hand in hand,
We create a world that's truly grand.

Illuminated Connections

Amidst the dark, we spark a flame,
Each little light, we share the same.
With whispered dreams, our hopes align,
In radiant circles, our hearts entwine.

Through every word, we weave our ties,
In unveiled truths, no need for guise.
As starlit skies glow overhead,
We journey forth, where joy is spread.

Together we dance in harmony,
Melodies forged in unity.
With laughter ringing, spirits soar,
Creating bonds that we adore.

In every glance, a story told,
In silver lines of friendship bold.
As paths converge, we find our place,
Embracing all, with warmth and grace.

Through trials faced, we carry on,
With every dawn, a brand-new song.
In these connections, we thrive,
A dance of hearts, forever alive.

The Glow Between Us

In twilight's hush, we meet anew,
With radiant smiles, our spirits brew.
A glow in hearts that brightly sings,
This bond we share, a gift it brings.

Through whispered thoughts and gentle touch,
We find in silence, oh so much.
In moments fleeting, we hold tight,
Creating memories, pure delight.

The world may shake, the winds may roar,
But in our hearts, we seek for more.
A lighthouse beam in darkest night,
Together we shine, a guiding light.

With every step, we dance as one,
A journey started, never done.
In laughter shared, a joyful play,
In this connection, come what may.

So let us treasure what we find,
In this embrace, our souls aligned.
For in the glow that passes through,
Exists a spark, forever true.

Harmony of Hearts

In perfect rhythm, our hearts beat,
Creating music, oh so sweet.
With every song, a tale unwind,
In harmony, we're intertwined.

Through seasons change, we navigate,
With open arms, we choose our fate.
Each note we play, a step we take,
In unity, our ground we stake.

A symphony of dreams we dare,
In laughter's echo, love's bright flare.
Bound by purpose, we stand our ground,
In tender moments, beauty found.

As distant stars, we shine above,
In every heartbeat, a song of love.
With courage fierce, we break the mold,
In harmony, our stories told.

So let the world hear our sweet refrain,
In every joy, in every pain.
For in this dance, we truly see,
The beauty of hearts in harmony.

Light Between Us

In shadows cast, we find our way,
A spark of hope that holds the day.
With every step, our hearts will trust,
In the warm glow, there's love for us.

Through whispered dreams, we'll weave the thread,
Where every word remains unsaid.
A gentle brush, a soft embrace,
Together trapped in timeless space.

The light we share, it knows no bounds,
In every silence, joy resounds.
With every beat, we rise and soar,
Together, we are evermore.

A beacon bright, our souls align,
In vibrant hues, our paths entwine.
The light between us, pure and true,
A guide through storm and skies of blue.

So hand in hand, let's face the night,
Embracing shadows, holding tight.
Through every challenge, we will fight,
For in our hearts, we hold the light.

Reflections of Unity

In mirrored depths, our voices blend,
As echoes dance and hearts transcend.
Together strong, we rise as one,
In unity, our fears undone.

The threads of fate, they intertwine,
Creating paths that brightly shine.
In every laugh, in every tear,
We forge a bond that draws us near.

With open eyes, we see the truth,
A tapestry of love and youth.
Through trials faced, we stand as friends,
In every story, hope transcends.

We find the strength in shared embrace,
In gathering storms, we find our place.
Reflecting light in darkest hours,
Together, we bloom like springtime flowers.

With each sunrise, our spirits grow,
In harmony, our hearts will glow.
Reflections bright in every glance,
In unity, we dare to dance.

Glimmers in the Dark

When night descends, we search for light,
In every corner, hope ignites.
A flicker here, a shimmer there,
In shadows deep, we find our prayer.

Through winding paths, we find our way,
With glimmers guiding, come what may.
Beyond the veil of doubt and fear,
We chase the whispers, drawing near.

The stars above, they softly guide,
In the gentle glow, we find our pride.
With hands united, we stand tall,
In glimmers bright, we will not fall.

For in the dark, our dreams take flight,
In every heartbeat, there's pure light.
Through trials faced, we hold the spark,
Together, we are brave and stark.

Embrace the glimmers, hold them tight,
For in our souls, we burn so bright.
Through darkest nights, we rise anew,
Together, we will push on through.

Harmony of Beams

In symphony, our voices blend,
A chorus that will never end.
With every note, our spirits soar,
In harmony, we ask for more.

The beams of light that guide our song,
In every right and every wrong.
Together we will find our way,
In rhythm's pulse, we dance and sway.

Each heart a string, a vibrant chord,
In love's embrace, we are restored.
Through laughter shared and tears that fall,
In harmony, we find our call.

With gentle whispers, dreams take flight,
Creating magic in the night.
For in this space, we are alive,
With every heartbeat, we will thrive.

In unity, our souls will gleam,
A dance of love, a shared dream.
Together bright, we'll chase the sun,
In harmony, we are as one.

A Tapestry of Rays

In morning light we rise anew,
Each ray a thread, a vibrant hue.
Together woven, hearts entwined,
A tapestry of dreams designed.

Bright whispers dance on sunlit streams,
In harmony, we chase our dreams.
With laughter shared and stories spun,
We paint the world, a canvas fun.

Under skies both blue and wide,
We walk the paths, our fears aside.
Each moment cherished, love expressed,
In every heartbeat, we are blessed.

As evening hues begin to glow,
We find our peace in twilight's show.
A tapestry of memories bright,
We hold each other through the night.

Shimmering Souls

In the quiet of the night,
We share our dreams, hearts take flight.
Like stars that dance in endless skies,
Our souls ignite, a bright surprise.

Through every laugh, through every tear,
We hold each other, always near.
A shimmering bond, too strong to break,
In each embrace, new memories make.

When darkness falls, we find the light,
In every heart, a spark ignites.
Together, we shine, a radiant glow,
In the tapestry of life we flow.

As whispers fade and night grows deep,
We carve our dreams in memories we keep.
Each shimmering soul a guiding star,
Together in unity, never far.

Collective Glow

In circles gathered, hands held tight,
Together we bask in shared delight.
Our laughter rises, a joyful call,
In this moment, we stand tall.

From distant places, we unite,
Our spirits mingling, pure and bright.
With every word, we weave the song,
In collective glow, we all belong.

The energy flows like a gentle stream,
With each heartbeat, we become a dream.
An infinite bond, strong and wide,
In harmony, we break the tide.

Through trials faced and joys we share,
Our hearts entwined, beyond compare.
In every glance, a spark we know,
Together we flourish, we are the glow.

Moonbeams of Togetherness

Beneath the moon's soft, silver light,
We gather close, hearts taking flight.
In shadows long, our laughter rings,
The joy of life, the warmth it brings.

With every story shared in peace,
Our bonds grow strong, sweet release.
Moonbeams dance upon our skin,
In this embrace, our light begins.

Through midnight's hush, we find our way,
Each whispered hope a brand-new day.
Together we explore the night,
In moonlit dreams, we take our flight.

As dawn approaches, we hold tight,
The love we share, a radiant light.
In every moment, forever blessed,
In moonbeams of togetherness, we rest.

A Shimmering Embrace

In the twilight's gentle glow,
Whispers dance upon the streams.
Waves reflect the moon's soft light,
Night wraps us in silver dreams.

Hands entwined, we find our way,
Through the shadows, side by side.
With each heartbeat, night holds sway,
In this magic, we confide.

Stars above begin to gleam,
Painting tales upon the sky.
In this stillness, we will dream,
Together, as the moments fly.

Nature sighs, the world stands still,
Every breath a sacred song.
In this place, we bend to will,
Here, my heart has found its home.

As dawn weaves through the veil of night,
Our souls retained in purest grace.
Forever held in softest light,
In this shimmering embrace.

Synchronized Illumination

In a dance of fate, we glow,
Your touch a spark igniting fire.
Together, hearts begin to know,
The rhythm of our deep desire.

Brighter than the sunlit morn,
Every glance a flick'ring flame.
In this bond, no heart is torn,
In this weave, we share the same.

Guided by the stars that shine,
Every promise sewn in time.
Our spirits lift in pure design,
Synchronized in perfect rhyme.

With each pulse, we light the dark,
Filling shadows with our grace.
Every heartbeat plays its part,
In this dance, we find our place.

Together we will chase the spark,
Through the night, forever bright.
In this life, where we embark,
Shining souls, our hearts take flight.

Together Under the Stars

Beneath a canopy of night,
We lay on blankets, dreams alight.
The universe unfolds its lore,
Together, we can seek for more.

Whispers in the cool night breeze,
Stories told with tender ease.
Galaxies blink, a cosmic gaze,
In their dance, we'll spend our days.

Our laughter rings like silver chimes,
Echoing through the starry climes.
In this moment, time stands still,
With every breath, we find our will.

Holding hands with fate in sight,
We embrace the endless night.
Hearts intertwined, souls at play,
Under the stars, we drift away.

In the stillness, dreams take flight,
Guided by the moon's soft light.
Together, endless journeys start,
Under the stars, we join our hearts.

Kinship in Light

In the glow of amber dawn,
We find each other, never gone.
Shared laughter warms the chilly air,
In this kinship, love laid bare.

Every moment feels so rare,
As we walk with hearts laid bare.
Through the darkness, we will shine,
With our spirits, so divine.

In the dance of day and night,
We gather warmth, we gather light.
Each glance a promise made in trust,
In this bond, it's love we must.

Hands held tight, we face the storm,
In the chaos, we find warm.
Side by side, we lift each other,
In this life, we are each other.

With every step, our shadows blend,
In this journey, we transcend.
Together, hearts forever bright,
In the kinship found in light.

Radiating Together

In the quiet dawn, we rise,
With dreams like the morning skies.
Hands intertwined, hearts aglow,
Sharing warmth, letting love flow.

In every whisper, sparks ignite,
Guiding us through the darkest night.
The world may dim, but we will shine,
A bond unbroken, yours and mine.

Through every storm, we stand tall,
Together we conquer, never fall.
With every laugh, we chase despair,
Creating magic, a love laid bare.

As seasons change, we'll stay aligned,
Finding beauty that's undefined.
In golden rays or silver hues,
Our rhythm plays, a timeless muse.

So let us dance, hearts in the sun,
Radiating light, two become one.
In unity's glow, forever found,
Our love, a beacon that knows no bounds.

Beams of Affection

Beneath the stars, we sit and dream,
In a world of glow, where soft lights beam.
Each smile shared, a treasure bright,
A canvas painted with pure delight.

In gentle whispers, hearts collide,
Architects of joy, love as our guide.
With every gaze, the warmth we feed,
Sowing kindness, planting a seed.

Through fleeting moments, time takes flight,
In a dance of beams, we hold on tight.
With laughter ringing through the air,
Our souls entwined, a radiant pair.

As daylight fades and shadows creep,
In embrace, our promises keep.
For in this space, affection grows,
A garden rich where passion flows.

In every sunset, in every dawn,
Our love's a fire, never gone.
With beams of affection, we remain,
Two hearts united through joy and pain.

The Luminescence of Us

In every heartbeat, a glow ignites,
The luminescence of our nights.
With laughter echoing through the years,
We cast away doubt, conquer fears.

Through moonlit paths, our spirits soar,
Together we've opened love's door.
With each new dawn, a brighter hue,
In shades of warmth, it's me and you.

Through every trial, hand in hand,
In harmony, together we stand.
A sacred dance under starlit skies,
In your embrace, my spirit flies.

As constellations light our way,
We weave our dreams, come what may.
In the stillness, our hearts trust,
Shining brightly, as love must.

With every sunset, our bond grows near,
In the luminescence, I hold you dear.
Together we'll glow, forever bright,
In the universe, our love is the light.

Flickering in Unison

In gentle flames, our hearts ignite,
Flickering softly, a shared light.
Together we dance, a fire's glow,
In warmth of love, we let it flow.

Through shadows deep, our spirits rise,
In the quiet moments, love never lies.
With every glance, a spark of grace,
In the flicker, I find my place.

As twilight falls and stars appear,
In unison, we conquer fear.
With every breath, the bond we weave,
In this glow, we will believe.

Through winds that howl and nights that chill,
In harmony, we find our will.
Together we shimmer, a perfect flame,
In the heart's whispers, calling your name.

As dreams take flight and night unfolds,
In the flicker of love, the story told.
Together we shine, a steadfast trust,
Flickering in unison, powerful and just.

Basking in Affinity

In the warmth of a shared embrace,
Connections bloom, heartbeats race.
Voices blend like sweet refrains,
Together we dance, free from chains.

Eyes meet under the golden light,
Whispers echo in the still of night.
Laughter rings like crystal chimes,
Creating memories, transcending times.

Hands entwined, we walk as one,
Tales of joy beneath the sun.
Every moment, a spark ignites,
In this bond, our love ignites.

As the stars begin to gleam,
We weave a never-ending dream.
Side by side, through thick and thin,
In our hearts, we always win.

So let the world fade away,
In our haven, here we stay.
Breathing life in harmony,
Forever basking, you and me.

Unified Sparks

When our eyes first met that day,
A rush of warmth swept us away.
In the silence, a language found,
Two hearts beating, a profound sound.

The hopes we share ignite the flame,
Together, we are never the same.
Through every trial, we stand so tall,
United in purpose, we give our all.

Moments rush like rivers flow,
In this dance, we learn to grow.
With every glance, the world is bright,
Our spirits soar, taking flight.

In whispers soft, our truths revealed,
We discover strength, our hearts unsealed.
Flickers of trust light up the night,
In a symphony of shared delight.

Together we dream, together we rise,
In the canvas of life, endless skies.
With every heartbeat, a promise we make,
Unified sparks, never to break.

Kindred Glows

In the twilight, where shadows play,
Kindred spirits find their way.
With every laugh, the air is sweet,
In this circle, love's heartbeat.

Through the storms that come and go,
We stand grounded, in kindred glow.
With open hearts, we share our fears,
In this bond, we wipe the tears.

As the sun sets, colors blend,
Together we share, no need to pretend.
Each moment cherished, every glance bright,
In this tapestry, we find our light.

With stories woven, hand in hand,
We create our dreams, a promised land.
Every sunset paints the sky anew,
In our hearts, a vibrant hue.

So let the world turn, let it spin,
With our kindred glow, we always win.
In every heartbeat, in every sigh,
Together forever, you and I.

Reflections of Affinity

In a mirror, our souls align,
Each reflection, a beautiful sign.
With every glance, we understand,
Together, we build, hand in hand.

Through the rough and through the clear,
Our laughter rises, washing fear.
With every tear, we softly mend,
In this journey, love will send.

Moments flicker like candlelight,
In your eyes, I find my sight.
Side by side, through ebb and flow,
In every heartbeat, affinity grows.

As seasons shift from bloom to fall,
In our hearts, we hear the call.
With open arms, we embrace the new,
Reflections of me, reflections of you.

So let us dance in fading light,
With every step, our spirits unite.
In this bond, let's write our song,
Together, forever, where we belong.

Chasing Light as One

In the dawn's embrace we rise,
With hope painted across the skies.
Together we shall run and dream,
Chasing light along the stream.

Through valleys low and hills so high,
Laughter echoes, spirits fly.
Hand in hand, we make our way,
In unity, we greet the day.

Every shadow holds its glow,
In every heart, a warmth we sow.
With every step, our path is bright,
Together shining, pure and right.

When storms may come to still our pace,
We'll find our strength, each other's grace.
As one, we'll weather all the strife,
Chasing light, we find our life.

In the twilight's gentle fold,
Memories forged in threads of gold.
As each day ends, our spirits sing,
Chasing light, forever spring.

The Fire of Fellowship

Around the flame, we gather close,
In warmth and laughter, we engross.
With stories shared, our hearts ignite,
The fire of fellowship burns bright.

Through trials faced and joys explored,
In unity, our spirits soared.
Each ember glows with kindred light,
Together we face the darkest night.

As shadows dance upon the ground,
In friendship's bond, true strength is found.
We fuel the flame with trust and love,
Guided by stars that shine above.

With every laugh, with every song,
In harmony, we all belong.
The fire crackles, spirits swell,
In this embrace, all is well.

For in this warmth, we find our way,
Through every night, into each day.
The fire of fellowship will stay,
A guiding light, come what may.

Glowing in Tandem

Like stars aligned in the vast night,
We shine together, hearts in flight.
With every breath, we intertwine,
Glowing in tandem, yours and mine.

In every moment, side by side,
In whispered dreams, our hopes collide.
Through trials faced, we boldly stand,
Together, we will take command.

When darkness falls, we light the way,
Our bond will guide, come what may.
Reflecting strength through every tear,
In harmony, we cast out fear.

Each journey shared, like paths of gold,
In stories cherished, we grow bold.
Glowing in tandem, we embrace,
In friendship's warmth, we find our place.

Across the miles, our spirits soar,
In every heartbeat, we explore.
With love as our eternal flame,
Glowing in tandem, we proclaim.

Luminous Threads of Life

In tapestry of dreams we weave,
With every thread, we dare believe.
In colors bright, our stories blend,
Luminous threads, on them we depend.

Through laughter shared and tears we've shed,
In every moment, love is spread.
Connected hearts, we dance and fly,
Binding us under the same sky.

Each memory holds a spark divine,
In every bond, our souls align.
In the fabric of the night, we glow,
Luminous threads in every flow.

As seasons shift, we stand as one,
Through every journey, life's begun.
With courage found in hands entwined,
Luminous threads, forever kind.

In this vast world, we find our place,
With every heartbeat, we embrace.
Together woven, rich and rife,
In luminous threads, we find our life.

Together We Shine

Hand in hand, we rise and sway,
In the light of a brand new day,
Hearts aligned, a gentle spark,
Together we ignite the dark.

With every laugh, our spirits soar,
Painting dreams, we long for more,
In the tapestry of time we weave,
Believe in what we can achieve.

Through stormy skies, we find our way,
In unity, we break the fray,
Guiding each other, side by side,
In each heartbeat, love abides.

Whispers echo in the night,
Each moment shared feels so right,
In the glow of friendship's fire,
We build our world, we reach higher.

Together we shine, a radiant beam,
Chasing shadows, we dare to dream,
For in our hearts, the brave define,
An everlasting bond, divine.

Luminous Connections

Flickering stars in boundless skies,
With every glance, a truth that lies,
In the warmth of a knowing glance,
Together we embrace the dance.

Threads of gold, woven with care,
In our stories, memories shared,
Echoing laughter, a harmonious song,
In the tapestry of us, we belong.

Distance fades, as hearts unite,
In dreamlike realms, we take flight,
Illuminated paths, bright and clear,
With every step, we draw near.

The pulse of love, steady and strong,
In every heart, a vital song,
The colors blend, a vibrant hue,
Celebrating the bond, ever new.

Luminous connections, shining bright,
In the dark, we find our light,
With open hearts, we dare to see,
A world where love will always be.

Interwoven Gleams

In the fabric of life, we find our thread,
Interwoven paths where dreams are fed,
With each breath, a new story blooms,
In every heart, hope resumes.

Whispers of joy fill the air,
Moments cherished, beyond compare,
Through laughter's echo, we understand,
Together, we craft a promised land.

Side by side, we conquer fears,
In the dance of time, we're pioneers,
Through trials faced, our spirits rise,
In the glow of love, we realize.

A tapestry rich with shared dreams,
In every soul, a gentle gleam,
Through life's journey, hand in hand,
We paint our dreams upon the sand.

Interwoven gleams, bright and true,
Crafting a world for me and you,
In every heartbeat, a story told,
In harmony, our lives unfold.

Brightened Paths

Beneath the stars, we make our way,
With every step, a brightening ray,
Through tangled woods, we find the light,
Guiding each other, holding tight.

In the quiet moments, we define,
The hopes we share, the love that shines,
Through valleys deep, we stand as one,
Each challenge faced, a victory won.

Voices gentle, like a song,
In our hearts, where we belong,
With every heartbeat, pathways glow,
In unity, our spirits flow.

With colors bold, we paint the skies,
Under the arch of endless ties,
Together we stand, bold and free,
Brightened paths for all to see.

The journey forward, hand in hand,
In the embrace of love, we stand,
With every step, our spirits soar,
In our brightened paths, forevermore.

Fusion of Lights

In twilight's embrace, colors dance,
A symphony of hues, a fleeting chance.
Whispers of warmth call out in the night,
Soft glimmers unite, creating delight.

Across the canvas, shadows play,
Each moment captured, then swept away.
In the fusion of lights, we find our way,
Creating memories that forever stay.

Stars twinkle softly, guiding our sight,
Illuminating paths, turning dark to bright.
In the stillness, a gentle sigh,
As dreams take flight beneath the sky.

Moments blend in the serene glow,
Where time stands still and secrets flow.
In the heartbeat of night, connection ignites,
Finding solace in fusion of lights.

Weaving together the threads of the day,
In the dance of dusk, they softly sway.
With every heartbeat, a rhythm divine,
In the fusion of lights, our spirits entwine.

Illuminating Moments

In the quiet dusk, a spark ignites,
Moments of joy, painting the nights.
Each laugh, each tear, a radiant sign,
Illuminating memories, endlessly intertwine.

The glow of friendship brightens the way,
A lighthouse guiding through shades of gray.
In the tapestry woven with every breath,
Illuminating moments, conquering death.

When the sun dips low and shadows grow,
The warmth of connection begins to flow.
In shared glances, where silence speaks,
Illuminating moments, solace it seeks.

With every heartbeat, the night unfurls,
A canvas of memories, it gently swirls.
Bathed in the glow of a thousand stars,
Illuminating moments, healing our scars.

As dawn breaks through, the memories stay,
Illuminating light to guide our way.
In every heartbeat, and every sigh,
These moments of bliss will never die.

Echoes of Illumination

Whispers of light in the stillness resound,
Echoes of memories found all around.
In the gentle glow, stories unfold,
Illuminating dreams, both timid and bold.

As shadows retreat, a soft sigh of peace,
In the echoing light, anxieties cease.
With each flicker, a promise is made,
Echoes of illumination, never to fade.

Through the corridors of time, we roam,
In the heart of the light, we find our home.
Each moment a whisper, soft and sincere,
Echoes of illumination, always near.

In the dance of dawn, colors embrace,
A symphony of light, a timeless grace.
As day claims the night, and shadows dissolve,
Echoes of illumination begin to evolve.

With every heartbeat, the memories shine,
In the tapestry of light, our souls align.
In the echoes of time, we find our place,
Echoes of illumination, woven with grace.

Simmering Amongst Stars

In the vast expanse where dreams ignite,
Simmering softly, amidst the night.
Every flicker, a heart's embrace,
Dancing together, a celestial pace.

Starlight whispers secrets, tender and bright,
Guiding us through, the velvety night.
With every shimmer, we come alive,
Simmering amongst stars, where hopes thrive.

In the silence, our wishes take flight,
Beneath the canvas, painted with light.
Held in the cosmos, a moment so rare,
Simmering amongst stars, free from despair.

With every heartbeat, the universe sways,
In the dance of the night, our spirit plays.
A symphony of starlight, softly weaves,
Simmering amongst stars, we believe.

As dawn approaches and shadows fade,
The glow of the night, memories made.
In the lingering warmth, our hearts stay,
Simmering amongst stars, come what may.

www.ingramcontent.com/pod-product-compliance
Lightning Source LLC
Chambersburg PA
CBHW070428230125
20710CB00012B/491